KT-452-835

Cooking the Mexican Way

LOURDES NICHOLS

A SAINSBURY COOKBOOK

Published by Woodhead-Faulkner Limited
17 Market Street, Cambridge CB2 3PA
for J Sainsbury plc
Stamford House, Stamford Street, London SE1 9LL

First published 1983
© J Sainsbury plc 1983

Conditions of sale
All rights reserved. No part of this publication may be reproduced,
stored in a retrieval system or transmitted, in any form or by any
means, electronic, mechanical, photocopying or otherwise, without
the prior permission of the copyright holders.

The publishers wish to thank the Mexican Tourist Board for their
help in supplying some of the items which appear in the
photographs.

Design and layout: Ken Vail Graphic Design
Photography: John Lee
Food preparation for photography: Ann Page-Wood
Illustrations: Chris Evans
Typesetting: Westholme Graphics Limited, Gamlingay, Beds
Origination: Anglia Reproductions, Witham, Essex
Printed and bound in Great Britain by
William Clowes (Beccles) Limited, Beccles and London

Contents

3

Introduction

Mexican food has taken the United States by storm in recent years and looks set to be equally popular in Great Britain. Although so far it has been mainly available here as take-away 'fast food', it is easy to cook in the kitchen at home and the result is far more likely to resemble genuine Mexican cooking.

It is not hard to see why Mexican food is becoming so popular: colourful and exciting, delicious and filling, exotic yet wholesome and economical, it is equally suited to family meals or dinner parties. A little meat often goes a long way in Mexican dishes, with a lot of the protein coming from beans and vegetables; this makes it not only very economical but also healthy. Although it can be spicy, most of the ingredients are familiar foods available anywhere and the 'hotness' can be adjusted easily to suit every taste. Preparation methods are very simple and many of the recipes will freeze very well for reheating at a later date – especially useful for modern life-styles.

What is the Mexican style of cookery? Many people would immediately think of *tortillas* (corn pancakes), beans and hot chilli flavouring as typical features. Although it is true that these ingredients, especially the tortillas, crop up often, I hope to show you in this book that there is much more than that to Mexican cuisine. A more important characteristic is the pride of place occupied by fresh vegetables and fruit. In nutritional terms, these contain a lot of health-giving vitamins and dietary fibre, which is one of the reasons that Mexican cookery fits in so well with modern ideas of a healthy diet.

The cooking in Mexico has been influenced by various European cuisines – Spanish, obviously, and to a lesser extent French – but its basis is still the native style, which goes back to the Aztecs and derives from the country's abundance of natural foods. Turkeys, peanuts, tomatoes, sweetcorn, avocado pears, pumpkins, courgettes, marrows, pineapples, many kinds of beans, chillies, chocolate and vanilla are all native products of Mexico that were introduced to Europe after the Spanish conquest; all of them feature again and again in Mexican dishes. The Aztecs used to cook their food by boiling, steaming or roasting over a wood fire. After the Spaniards introduced the pig and its much-appreciated fat, frying became a popular method. Ovens were almost unknown and are not common in Mexican kitchens even now; however, I have adapted recipes where necessary to take account of the conveniences of a modern British kitchen – oven and blender rather than open fire and pestle-and-mortar!

A typical day's meals in Mexico today would begin with a breakfast of fresh fruit juice, eggs cooked in many different ways accompanied by warm tortillas or fresh bread, and black coffee or chocolate. That is in the cities; in the countryside the peasants will go to work at dawn after a meal of black coffee and tortillas, returning at about ten o'clock for *almuerzo* (brunch), consisting of eggs, beans, tortillas and more coffee. The humble peasant needs no plates or cutlery but wraps his food in a freshly made, warm tortilla, and even the most sophisticated and affluent town-dweller will eat his tortilla the traditional way, 'by hand'.

The main meal everywhere is in the middle of the day, at around two o'clock. A typical lunch would include soup, 'dry soup' (rice or pasta in sauce), meat with one vegetable, beans, salad, and fruit or dessert accompanied by black coffee. (Mexican cookery is not noted for its desserts: although the Spaniards introduced milk and sugar, fresh tropical fruit is still the typical light, sweet end to a meal.) Tortillas are offered throughout this succession of courses, as well as some sort of *salsa* (sauce) to make *tacos* with (see p. 71). In some homes white bread, usually freshly baked and resembling small French rolls, called *bolillos* or *teleras*, is offered. *Agua fresca* (cool, fruit-flavoured water) is always available.

After such a heavy lunch, supper is a light meal. Served at about eight or nine o'clock, it usually takes the form of an *antojito* (a 'little whim', i.e. whatever takes your fancy). Beans with soft tortillas or sweet bread and hot chocolate or coffee are very popular.

In this book I have provided a sample of typically Mexican recipes which I am sure will turn you into an enthusiast for this exciting national cuisine. They are all my personal versions of genuine Mexican dishes, with just the occasional ingredient adapted to what is available in Britain. They range from starters to desserts, and I have included some suggestions for authentic Mexican drinks.

Ingredients

Exact combinations of ingredients have never been a feature of the Mexican cuisine. Because it is centuries old and has been passed down from one generation to another by word of mouth, small changes and adjustments have always been the accepted norm. The amounts of salt, black pepper, chillis and some spices given in the recipes in this book are only a rough guide, for my aim is to inspire you to experiment and do what tastes right to you. After all, that is half the fun of cooking – especially Mexican cooking!

Avocado pears (*Aguacates*) Avocado pears come in many different sizes, colours and textures. In Mexico they are available the whole year round. The small, black-skinned ones that resemble a large plum are my favourites.

Avocado pears are eaten hot only when dropped into soup before serving, or when made into avocado soup. The use of fresh coriander and lime with them accentuates their mild flavour.

Always remember to buy avocado pears at least five days in advance during the winter months; in the summer months, two or three days ahead will be sufficient. Avocado pears sold in Britain are not normally ripe enough to eat the same day.

You can tell that an avocado is ripe when it gives slightly, like a peach, if pressed gently between your fingers. To ripen, wrap in newspaper and keep in a warm room or airing cupboard. Check daily, turning round for even ripening. If an avocado seems ripe before you are ready to use it, you may delay its maturity by placing it in the vegetable compartment of your refrigerator.

Beans (*Frijoles*) Beans are pulses of different colours and sizes which constitute the main source of protein in the Mexican diet. They are rich in minerals and protein and are eaten at every meal. Amongst the better known in Britain are the red kidney beans. They must first be soaked to allow them to swell and soften and then boiled at a rolling boil until very soft; this can take 2–3 hours.

In Mexico beans are cooked in an earthenware pot and are boiled continuously for up to 3 hours. Boil for at least 15 minutes to extract the substances which can cause stomach pains. Always check to ensure they are boiling in sufficient water, enough to cover them at least 2 inches (5 cm) over the top. *Never* add cold water to boiling beans or the result will be *frijoles parados* – 'standing-up beans' – which are indigestible and unpalatable.

Beans are a tasty and economical way of feeding the family. One pound (450 g) of dried beans yields approximately 3 lb (1.35 kg) of cooked beans. Beans are amongst the most popular dishes in Mexico and together with maize and chillies they make a happy trio providing daily protein, carbohydrate and vitamin C requirements.

It is advisable not to serve more than one bean dish at each meal, as beans cause flatulence and can make some people extremely uncomfortable. However, the more often you eat them the less they have this effect on you.

Chillies (*Chiles*) Chillies are eaten both raw and cooked. Their pungency is variable, but some are so hot that they will irritate your fingers (or your eyes, if you rub them with your fingers) for days. To avoid getting 'hot fingers' you should wear rubber gloves or use a knife and fork to handle chillies; chop them on an absorbent kitchen towel.

To control the amount of 'sting' in your dish follow these simple rules:

(*a*) For mild dishes do not prick or puncture a chilli; leave it whole. Remove chillies from dishes immediately after the cooking is finished.

(*b*) For medium-hot dishes, add several whole chillies, then slice only one lengthways, discarding the seeds.

(*c*) For hot dishes, add sliced chillies, seeds and all. Keep in mind that not everyone has the same tolerance and once your dish is 'hot' there is little you can do to make it mild. Taste as you add more chillies so that you know when to stop.

The basic ingredients of Mexican cooking are, with very few exceptions, readily available in British shops and supermarkets

(*d*) For use in uncooked dishes, like Salcita and Guacamole, I generally chop the chillies as fine as I can so that when they are mixed with the other ingredients no one will get an overdose!

To be on the safe side, I always prepare 'pickled peppers' (see p. 31) and place them on the table separately, while keeping the chillies actually cooked in the dish to a minimum. In this way each person can regulate the amount they dare take. If you have never been exposed to chillies and would like to try them, all I can say is take a little piece of chilli at a time with a forkful of food.

To keep chillies, remove the stalks carefully so that you do not break the fruit, wrap the fruit in absorbent kitchen paper and refrigerate in an airtight container. They will keep well for about two weeks. Do not freeze chillies.

Recipes calling for Mexican varieties of dry chillies have deliberately been omitted from this book because they are almost impossible to obtain in this country.

Coriander (*Cilantro*)   Coriander is used fresh in all recipes in this book (coriander seeds are seldom used in Mexican cooking). It is a herb which looks like parsley and is usually sold with its roots. It has such a distinct flavour when eaten raw that there is really no substitute for it. However, alternative herbs are possible in cooked dishes and I have specified these in the recipes.

Coriander keeps best wrapped in absorbent paper, and refrigerated in an airtight container it will keep for about ten days. If it seems a little limp, soak it in cold water for an hour, or remove the leaves from the stalks and soak them for 30 minutes before using. Do not freeze.

Quantities

Ingredients in the recipes are given in both imperial (oz, pints, etc) and metric (g, ml, etc) measures: use either set of quantities, but not a mixture of both, in any one recipe. All spoons are level unless otherwise stated; metric spoon measures are always level. Egg size, where unspecified, is medium (size 3). *NB* I have not given instructions in the recipes for removing seeds for chillies and peppers, since whether you remove them or not depends on how hot you want the dish to be – see previous notes on chillies.

Basic Recipes

Certain basic dishes are required again and again as ingredients or components of many of the recipes in this book. I have put them together in this section, to make them easier to find if you are preparing them fresh for a particular dish. However, I recommend you save time by making up a larger quantity and freezing for future use as needed (only the raw tomato sauce, p. 23, cannot be stored in this way).

Tortillas are the basis of very many recipes. Cooked or refried beans can be used both as ingredients and as accompanying dishes in their own right, as can the savoury minced beef recipe. The two tomato sauces and the avocado dip are delicious and versatile ingredients.

Tortillas

Tortilla was the name given by the Spaniards to the flat corn pancakes eaten by the Indians in Mexico. The primitive name was *tlaxcali*, because it was the Indians from the township of Tlaxcala who made them originally. Tortillas made the traditional way are patted by hand, one at a time, and lots of patience and rhythm are essential to keep the dough from folding or, indeed, dropping on the ground! Tortilla presses are a wonderfully simple solution to those of us who cannot get the rhythm right. They are used in many Mexican homes to speed up the process of tortilla making and are practical even if you only use them occasionally – though with practice a lot more can be achieved. The diagram overleaf shows how easy it is to make one for home use.

Tortillas must never be eaten cold, unless they are deep-fried and used as corn chips, called *totopos*. In every other case you should warm tortillas before serving them. They are most commonly eaten with savoury fillings, but are also offered to children warm with butter and sugar. They are used for appetisers, in soups and main courses and they take the place of bread at each meal. You need never throw a tortilla away, because there is always some use for a stale one.

I have provided two recipes for tortillas. The first one is for the traditional corn tortilla, for which you will need maize flour or *masa harina*: it is now available over here in speciality shops. The second recipe is for the rarer, but still authentic, wheat flour version, which uses ingredients that are more familiar and easier to come by in Britain. When you make tortillas, make a large batch and freeze plenty for future use.

Tortillas. In the background, a corn tortilla formed in a home-made tortilla press; maize flour (masa harina) is in the bowl. The larger cooked tortillas are wheat flour, the smaller, in the foreground, corn

Tortillas de Maiz

Corn tortillas

Makes approx. 30 tortillas, 6 inches (15 cm) in diameter

Corn tortillas are round, flat unleavened pancakes made of a mixture of specially prepared cornmeal and water. They are traditionally patted by hand until they are wafer-thin, then cooked on a hot griddle without grease or fat. In Mexico tortillas are bought by the kilo at the *tortillerías* but in Britain they are harder to find. They are available frozen or canned from speciality shops, but it is more satisfying to make your own.

This recipe must be followed exactly, otherwise you may find it very difficult to make the tortillas. If your first batch isn't entirely successful, persevere, making sure that you are keeping to the recipe; it's worth the trouble. A tortilla press is essential and you will need also a griddle or thick-bottomed frying pan and 40 squares of waxed paper, about 8 × 8 inches (20 × 20 cm).

1¼ lb (550 g) masa harina (maize flour)
4 oz (100 g) plain white flour
1 pint (525 ml) hot water

Place a heavy frying pan or griddle on medium heat and warm until a drop of water in it sizzles. In the meantime, mix the flours and add the water gradually, mixing as you go along. Knead as for bread, for 5 minutes with an electric mixer or 10 minutes by hand; you cannot over-knead the masa. You will know the dough is ready when a small ball placed in a glass of cold water does not dissolve.

Take 1 heaped tablespoon (2 × 15 ml spoon) of dough and mould it into a small ball in the palm of your hands. Open the tortilla press and place one square of waxed paper on the base of it, waxed side up.

Place the dough ball in the centre of the paper, a little nearer the bracket than the centre. Now put another square of waxed paper, waxed side down, over it. Fold the tortilla press down on it and apply pressure on the lever, gently pressing with your right hand and holding the top of the lever with your left hand.

Open the press and check the thickness of the tortilla: it should be no thicker than a penny. If it is too thick, close the press again and apply a little more pressure, turning the tortilla around a quarter turn. Peel off the top layer of paper, and hold the tortilla in your hand with the other layer of paper. Place it face down on the hot griddle and leave it for about a minute, when you may peel the paper off and save it to re-use later.

When the tortilla is cooked, the sides will start lifting. Turn it over and cook for half a minute, then turn a third time, pressing gently in the centre so that it bubbles up. Remove it from the heat and stack it with the other cooked tortillas, covered with a clean kitchen towel. They are now ready to eat, freeze or refrigerate.

Hints   If the tortillas come out of the press with ragged edges, the dough is too dry. Add a little more water to the dough, knead it a little longer, then try again. If the tortilla is too difficult to flatten, the same applies.

When the dough is too wet, the tortilla becomes very sticky; it will make a lot of bubbles when placed on the griddle and often will stick. Add a little more masa harina and knead a little longer until your hands are clean.

If the tortillas crack when cooked, the griddle is too cold; if they get black spots, the griddle is too hot. Cool it down by placing a saucepan of cold water over it.

To refrigerate   Allow tortillas to cool and then wrap them in a plastic bag, tying them securely with a freezer wire. Can be stored refrigerated for about one week.

To freeze   Wrap in a plastic bag, securely sealed, and place in a freezer; they will store for up to six months. They do not need to be thawed before use, as they do not stick together and so can easily be separated with the end of a knife and put straight on to a hot griddle. They will keep in a refrigerator for a week after thawing.

To reheat If you only need a few, warm up a griddle or heavy-bottomed frying pan until water sizzles on it. Place one tortilla on the griddle or pan at a time and heat for about 30 seconds on each side. Keep the tortillas warm in a clean napkin and serve as soon as possible.

If you need to warm up a lot of tortillas simultaneously, then make small parcels of 12 tortillas each, wrapped securely in aluminium foil. Place the parcels in a medium-hot oven (Gas Mark 5/375°F/190°C) for 15 minutes. Alternatively, bring the water in a double boiler to the boil and place all the wrapped tortillas in it, cover and allow to steam for 12 minutes. For microwave heating, wrap two tortillas in a cloth napkin and warm at high setting for 20 seconds.

To shallow-fry Cover the bottom of a heavy-bottomed frying pan with 1 inch (2 cm) of cooking oil. When the oil is hot, fry one tortilla at a time for about 20 seconds. Remove from the oil and drain on absorbent kitchen paper until required.

To deep-fry Heat at least 4 inches (10 cm) of oil in a deep fryer, to a temperature of 400°F/200°C as for potato chips. Immerse the tortillas and fry for 1–1½ minutes. With practice you may fry four or five tortillas at once if they are whole. Remove from the oil when they are light golden, as they keep browning after they have been removed. Drain on absorbent kitchen towels and eat cold.

To fry Totopos (see recipe on p. 44), you may fry as many as your fryer will hold, but make sure to stir them so they fry evenly.

Tortillas de Harina de Trigo

Wheat flour tortillas
Makes approx. 18 tortillas, 9 inches (24 cm) in diameter

Wheat flour tortillas are larger than corn tortillas and they come from northern Mexico, where maize does not grow so easily. They are made with animal fat, salt and plain white flour. Cooked on a hot griddle, they must be very pliable and soft for storage. For most purposes flour tortillas can be used in place of corn tortillas, and many people prefer them. They should be treated in the same manner and never eaten cold. To store flour tortillas you have to place waxed paper between them, as they tend to stick together, especially when frozen. They defrost easily if left at room temperature for 30 minutes.

1 tablespoon (15 ml spoon) salt
1 lb (450 g) plain flour
3 oz (75 g) lard or vegetable shortening
10 fl oz (275 ml) warm water (at body temperature)

Heat up a heavy-bottomed frying pan (without greasing it) on moderate heat until a drop of water in it sizzles. Sieve the salt and flour together, and blend in the fat as you would for ordinary pastry. Add warm water slowly – the amount may vary with the type of flour used, but only by a teaspoon (5 ml spoon) or two.

Knead the dough on a floured board with floured hands until it is no longer sticky, but is not hard. Keep the dough covered with a warm, damp cloth. Take approximately 1½ oz (35 g) dough at a time and knead, folding it back on itself to trap air for a few seconds. Now make it into a little ball and flatten it. Place the flattened ball on a floured board, and roll it out with a floured rolling pin until it is so thin that you can see the board through the pastry. Cut out the tortillas by placing a 9-inch (24 cm) plate on the thin dough and cutting around it.

Pick up each tortilla, lay it on your right hand and place it carefully on the moderately hot griddle or pan, making sure it is flat and has no folds. As it cooks it will thicken slightly and small bubbles will appear. Cook for about 40 seconds on one side and then turn it and cook it for about 30 seconds on the other side. When cooked it should feel heavy and floppy, soft and pliable.

Stack the cooked tortillas together, wrapped in a clean tea towel. Always eat them hot except when they have been fried, when they can be eaten cold if consumed within 4 hours. Flour tortillas are reheated in the same way as corn tortillas (see p. 16).

Frijoles
Beans
Makes approx. 2 pints (1.2 litres)

Beans are a staple in the Mexican diet, and so never hesitate to serve them as an accompaniment to Mexican dishes, whatever your choice of menu. The preparation starts two days before because they need to soak overnight and because they taste better the day after they are cooked. Since beans take a long time to cook, I suggest you cook 1 lb (450 g) at a time and freeze what you do not need.

1 lb (450 g) dried red kidney, black or pinto beans
2 cloves of garlic, skewered on a cocktail stick
2 teaspoons (2 × 5 ml spoon) salt
2 teaspoons (2 × 5 ml spoon) sugar
2 tablespoons (2 × 15 ml spoon) cooking oil
½ medium onion, chopped finely
2 whole green chillies

Examine the beans carefully for small stones, which are sometimes mixed in and are real tooth-breakers. Wash the beans in a strainer under the tap until the water is clear. Soak in water overnight, allowing about 5 inches (12 cm) of water above the level of the beans. (If you have forgotten to soak the beans overnight, you can put them in cold water, bring them to the boil and boil for 15 minutes and then soak them for just an hour.)

When ready to cook, add the garlic and boil the beans at a rolling boil for up to 3 hours or until they feel very soft between the fingers. They need to be topped up with boiling water frequently. Discard the garlic cloves, then add the salt and sugar and simmer gently for 10 minutes.

In the meantime, heat the cooking oil and sauté the onion until golden. Add to the beans, with the oil. Add the chillies, simmer for another 15 minutes and then discard the chillies. If the liquid looks very watery, mash some beans against the side of the pot to thicken the mixture and simmer for a little longer.

Cool and refrigerate until required (for up to 8 days). To serve, place the beans in a casserole and cover. Heat in a medium-hot oven, Gas Mark 4/350°F/180°C, for about 30 minutes. To freeze, cool and pack in airtight containers. To serve, thaw at room temperature for about 2 hours and heat as above or re-fry (see next recipe).

Frijoles Refritos

Re-fried beans
Makes approx. 1¼ lb (500 g); serves 4

In Mexico beans are served at each meal and are re-fried at each serving. In fact, re-fried beans become tastier with each frying as the flavour is intensified. Do make sure, however, that the other dishes in your menu are not too dry, as re-fried beans are about the consistency of mashed potatoes. This dish is a versatile filling or accompaniment and is suggested for use in many other recipes in this book.

2 tablespoons (2 × 15 ml spoon) cooking oil
½ onion, half sliced thickly and the other half chopped finely for garnish
1 pint (600 ml) cooked beans (half the preceding Frijoles recipe)

Heat the oil in a large heavy frying pan, and fry the thick slices of onion in it until dark brown. Discard the onion and add the beans, mashing them with a potato masher whilst they fry.

Keep stirring the beans as they tend to stick to the bottom and sides of the pan and could burn. If they do stick, make a hole in the centre and add 1 tablespoon (15 ml spoon) of oil at a time as required.

When the beans are the consistency of thick porridge, they are good for spreading over tortillas or bread. If you like them really dry, keep stirring until you can toss them in the air in the frying pan as you would a pancake.

If serving as an accompaniment, garnish with the reserved onion and serve hot with Totopos (see p. 44).

If you need to re-fry the beans yet again, use a little water to soften them first.

Frijoles and (in the foreground) Frijoles Refritos

Picadillo

Savoury minced meat filling
Makes approx. 1½ lb (675 g); serves 8

Picadillo is the common name for minced meat. It is often served with white rice but is also a very versatile filling for Empanadas (p. 74), Tacos (p. 71) and Chiles Rellenos (p. 72).

½ lb (225 g) minced beef
½ lb (225 g) minced pork
1 tablespoon (15 ml spoon) malt vinegar
¼ teaspoon (1.25 ml spoon) salt
a pinch of ground black pepper
a pinch of sugar
2 tablespoons (2 × 15 ml spoon) cooking oil
1 onion, chopped finely
1 clove of garlic, chopped finely
1 green pepper, chopped
2 green chillies, chopped finely (optional)
1 chicken stock cube
1 potato, cooked and diced
18 stuffed olives
2 tablespoons (2 × 15 ml spoon) flaked almonds
2 tablespoons (2 × 15 ml spoon) raisins
3 tablespoons (3 × 15 ml spoon) tomato purée
½ pint (300 ml) water

Season the meats with the vinegar, salt and black pepper and add the pinch of sugar.

Heat the oil in a heavy frying pan and sauté the onion, garlic, pepper and chillies. Add the meats and fry, stirring frequently, for about 10–15 minutes until the mixture starts to brown. Discard the surplus oil, taking care not to pour away the meat juices.

Add all other ingredients and simmer gently for about 15 minutes, stirring occasionally until the mixture starts to dry. Eat hot, unless using as a filling in Empanadas (p. 74), when it should be allowed to cool first. Picadillo can be refrigerated or frozen.

Salcita de Jitomate

Raw tomato sauce
Makes approx. 1 pint (600 ml)

This is an excellent sauce to use as filling for soft warm tortillas. You can also use it as a topping for Taco Shells (p. 71) or as a colourful side dish with a meal. This sauce does not keep, however, either frozen or refrigerated; it must be eaten within 4 hours of preparation.

8 ripe, firm tomatoes, chopped finely
15 sprigs of fresh coriander, chopped finely
1 onion, chopped finely
4 green chillies, chopped very finely (optional)
juice of 1 lime or lemon
1 teaspoon (5 ml spoon) salt
½ teaspoon (2.5 ml spoon) ground black pepper

Simply mix all the ingredients together thoroughly, 20 minutes before eating if possible. Serve cold.

Salsa de Jitomate

Cooked tomato sauce
Makes 1½ pints (900 ml)

This is a handy basic sauce which is very simple but tasty. It is present in most Mexican dishes and excellent to cook in bulk, as it freezes very well. It is used in a variety of main course dishes and snacks, and can even be used with spaghetti bolognese, lasagna and pizza. In Mexico fresh tomatoes would be charred, peeled and mashed, but canned peeled tomatoes are much more economical in Britain, and the flavour is just as good.

1 onion, chopped finely
2 tablespoons (2 × 15 ml spoon) cooking oil
2 × 1 lb 3 oz (539 g) can of peeled tomatoes
2 tablespoons (2 × 15 ml spoon) tomato purée (optional)
2 whole green chillies
1 chicken stock cube
a pinch of ground black pepper
a pinch of sugar

Sauté the onions in the hot oil. Liquidise the tomatoes and juice in a blender and add to the onions, along with the rest of the ingredients. Simmer gently for 15 minutes or until the chillies are soft.

If you do not want your sauce hot, remember to remove the chillies before storing. If you like it hot, slice the chillies, tasting as you go to control the amount of 'sting'.

Guacamole

Avocado dip (pictured on p. 45)
Makes approx. 1 pint (600 ml)

Guacamole is one of the most famous of Mexican dishes. *Mole* is the Nahuatl word for sauce and *guaca* stands for the shape of the avocado pear. Guacamole makes a delicious hors d'oeuvre or side dish, as well as an ingredient in many of the other recipes.

4 ripe, firm tomatoes, chopped finely
10 sprigs of fresh coriander, chopped finely
½ onion, chopped finely
2 green chillies, chopped very finely (optional)
juice of 1 lime or lemon
1 teaspoon (5 ml spoon) salt
½ teaspoon (2.5 ml spoon) ground black pepper
1 large, ripe avocado

Mix the tomatoes, coriander, onion, chillies, half the lime or lemon juice, salt and pepper together not more than half an hour before required.

Half an hour later, cut the avocado in half and spoon out the flesh, scraping the skin thoroughly to get the strong green colour. Mash it with a fork and mix into the tomato mixture.

To help stop the mixture from going brown, immerse the avocado stone in it. Smooth the surface and pour the remaining lime or lemon juice all over; then cover with cling film.

Just before serving, remove the cling film, pour off the extra lime or lemon juice and stir the mixture. If using as a starter, serve in a bowl surrounded by Totopos (see recipe on p. 44); the recipe will serve six in this way.

Antojitos
Light meals

Antojitos literally means 'little whims', i.e. 'what you fancy'. They are so irresistible that whether you are hungry or not you're bound to develop an appetite at whatever time of the day or night you smell these freshly cooked savouries. They are sold in markets and on street corners and are almost the Mexican equivalent of fish and chips, but in a hundred different varieties.

For family cooking, antojitos are outstanding. They are quick to prepare, satisfying and a great way to use leftovers. Antojitos are usually accompanied by Guacamole, Salcita de Jitomate (see previous section) or soured cream, with chopped lettuce and finely chopped raw onion for garnish. Often they are used as *bocadillos* (hors d'oeuvres) before a meal. For cocktail parties, which are now creeping into the Mexican way of life, many of the traditional antojitos are made bite-size.

Quesadillas

Cheese-filled tortillas
Serves 4

This is a popular snack which can be glorified and turned into a light lunch by serving it hot with re-fried beans and a sauce. It is extremely palatable to British people, who already have such a strong liking for cheese.

8 corn tortillas or 4 wheat flour tortillas
4 oz (100 g) mild Cheddar cheese, grated
½ onion, sliced finely into rings
2 green chillies, cut in strips (optional)

Heat a griddle or heavy frying pan until it sizzles when a few drops of water are sprinkled on it. Lay a tortilla on the hot surface and arrange about 1 oz (25 g) of grated cheese over it to cover, followed by one or two onion rings and some chilli strips if desired. Now place another tortilla on top, and leave on a medium heat for 1½ minutes.

When the cheese starts to melt, carefully turn the Quesadilla over and leave it for one more minute. When the cheese is nicely melted, remove it from the heat and serve immediately.

If you wish to prepare a large number at once, make parcels of about 12 tortillas wrapped together in aluminium foil. Place one foil parcel at a time in a double boiler and steam for 15 minutes. Unwrap and spread each half of a tortilla with cheese, onion and chilli if used, fold in half whilst still hot and secure with a cocktail stick.

When all the tortillas have been steamed and filled, place them on a baking tray, wrap in aluminium foil and leave until required. To reheat them, place them, still well wrapped, in a moderate oven (Gas Mark 4/350°F/180°C) for 15 minutes, until the cheese melts. Serve immediately.

Suggested accompaniments are Frijoles Refritos (recipe on p. 20) and either Salcita de Jitomate (p. 23) or Guacamole (p. 25).

Burritos

Wheat flour tortillas with a filling
Serves 6–8

This dish, which has been christened by the Americans and means literally 'little donkeys', is deservedly popular. The filling, like that for corn tortillas, may be just about any meat or vegetable, egg or beans. Try the following recipe first, then improvise with whatever filling you fancy. Fresh chopped onions and lettuce plus a sauce such as Guacamole will go well with any filling.

6–8 wheat flour tortillas
1 tablespoon (15 ml spoon) cooking oil
1 onion, sliced
1¼ lb (500 g) Frijoles Refritos (recipe on p. 20)
1 small lettuce, shredded finely
3 ripe tomatoes, sliced thinly
6 spring onions, chopped finely
8 oz (225 g) mild Cheddar cheese, grated finely
12 tablespoons (12 × 15 ml spoon) Guacamole (recipe on p. 25) or
    the same amount of Salcita (recipe on p. 23)

Heat the tortillas wrapped in aluminium foil in a medium-hot oven, Gas Mark 2/300°F/150°C, for 10 minutes just to make them pliable.

Heat the oil and sauté the onion. Then add the beans and stir for about 5 minutes until they are nice and hot.

Put 2 tablespoons (2 × 15 ml spoon) in the centre of each tortilla, sprinkle with the lettuce and add tomato slices, spring onions and cheese. Fold it like a parcel and secure with one or more cocktail sticks.

Put the Burritos in an ovenproof dish, cover them with aluminium foil very securely and heat them for 20 minutes in a medium oven, Gas Mark 4/350°F/180°C. Before serving lace with the Guacamole or Salcita.

Burritos, before and after 'parcelling'

Tortas

Mexican sandwiches
Serves 4

Tortas are the Mexican answer to sandwiches, but they are much more elaborate and one is usually enough for a light lunch. The most popular Mexican Tortas are made in *Torterias*, a type of take-away shop. The bread used is called *telera*, which is similar to a large crusty bun or a piece of a crusty French stick. In Mexico the bread is usually baked before each meal, but you can simply wrap it in foil and warm it in a moderate oven for about 15 minutes. The fillings can be as varied as you like, although the following mixture is delicious.

1 French stick (baguette size) cut into four, or 4 large crusty rolls
8 oz (225 g) Frijoles Refritos (recipe on p. 20)
4 slices of processed cheese, ham, cooked chicken or cold pork
½ lettuce, shredded finely
½ onion, sliced finely into rings
2 tomatoes, sliced finely
1 avocado, sliced
4 tablespoons (4 × 15 ml spoon) soured cream
Chiles en Vinagre (see following recipe), optional

Cut each roll or piece of bread in half and remove the centre. Spread the bottom with the warm re-fried beans and then top with a slice of cheese or meat, some lettuce, some onion rings and tomato slices, a slice or two of avocado and a tablespoon (15 ml spoon) of soured cream. Top with pickles, if desired, and replace the hollowed-out top piece of bread.

Chiles en Vinagre

Pickled peppers
Makes 2 pints (1.2 litres)

These pickles go particularly well with cheese and are also good in sandwiches, especially the Tortas in the preceding recipe and the Tostadas in the next recipe. They will keep very well in the refrigerator but remember to try only a little at a time!

6 tablespoons (6 × 15 ml spoon) cooking oil
12 green chillies, sliced thinly
4 large carrots, peeled and sliced thinly into rounds
2 large onions, sliced thinly
1 red pepper, sliced thinly
1 pint (600 ml) distilled malt vinegar
2 cloves of garlic, chopped finely
¼ teaspoon (1.25 ml spoon) oregano
¼ teaspoon (1.25 ml spoon) marjoram
¼ teaspoon (1.25 ml spoon) thyme
1 teaspoon (5 ml spoon) salt
½ teaspoon (2.5 ml spoon) ground black pepper
1 tablespoon (15 ml spoon) granulated sugar

Avoid handling the chillies with your bare hands, or you'll have 'hot' fingers for days – especially noticeable when you rub your nose, eyes or skin! Wear kitchen gloves or at least handle the chillies with respect; use a knife and fork, and cut them over kitchen paper towels which you discard afterwards.

Heat the oil in a large saucepan and toss the chillies, carrots, onions and red pepper for 2 minutes each, removing them from the heat and setting them aside in a bowl until they are all done. Slowly add the vinegar, herbs, seasoning and sugar to the oil and boil until the liquid is reduced by one-third. Pour the boiling liquid over the vegetables and allow to cool uncovered. When cold, transfer to clean jars and seal. Refrigerate once a jar is opened.

Tostadas

Fried crisp corn tortillas piled with salad
Serves 8

Tostadas are very popular throughout Mexico, and the filling varies according to the area: it can be crab, chicken, beef, pork, turkey or just salad. Whatever the filling, it is very colourful and is piled up until it looks like a little pyramid – almost impossible to eat, but Mexicans love pyramids, so why not join them!

8 corn tortillas
oil for deep frying
½ lb (225 g) Frijoles Refritos (recipe on p. 20)
½ lettuce, shredded finely
2 cooked chicken breasts, shredded finely
4 tomatoes, sliced finely
½ onion, sliced into rings
1 avocado, sliced
8 tablespoons (8 × 15 ml spoon) soured cream
2 oz (50 g) mild Cheddar cheese, grated
Chiles en Vinagre (see previous recipe)
salt and black pepper

Deep-fry the tortillas in the oil and warm the re-fried beans. Spread each tortilla with the warm beans and then lay on some of the lettuce, chicken, tomato, onion and avocado slices.

Spoon 1 tablespoon (15 ml spoon) of the soured cream over each Tostada. Sprinkle with cheese and add pickled peppers and a pinch of salt and black pepper. Eat immediately.

To eat, lift the whole Tostada with your hand, making sure you do not tilt it. Take a small bite at a time so you don't crack it and cause it all to drop on to your plate! You might also end up with a never-ending mouthful, if you attempt big bites. Serve one per person as a snack or two or more for a light meal.

Tortas (left) and Tostadas, with a jar of Chiles en Vinagre

Moyetes

Crusty rolls spread with beans
Serves 4

Moyetes are often served for breakfast and are very popular instead of bread and butter as an accompaniment to egg dishes.

4 crusty rolls
1 oz (25 g) butter
8 oz (225 g) Frijoles Refritos (recipe on p. 20)
2 oz (50 g) mild Cheddar cheese, grated
¼ onion, chopped finely

Cut each roll in half and remove some of the soft inside. Spread with butter and some of the re-fried beans and sprinkle them with cheese and raw onion. Bake in a moderate oven, Gas Mark 2/300°F/150°C, for 15–20 minutes. Eat hot.

Huevos Rancheros

Ranch-style eggs
Serves 4

Huevos Rancheros are a good example of a Mexican almuerzo ('brunch') dish and are suitable for a light lunch or supper.

16 corn tortillas or 8 wheat flour tortillas
oil for deep frying
8 oz (225 g) Frijoles Refritos (recipe on p. 20)
8 eggs
1 pint (600 ml) Salsa de Jitomate (recipe on p. 24)

Deep-fry the tortillas in very hot oil. If they puff up as they fry, press them flat with a kitchen spoon. Drain on absorbent kitchen paper and keep warm.

Warm the beans and spread them over the fried tortillas. Fry the eggs and place them on top of the beans, then spoon the hot tomato sauce over them.

Enfrijoladas

Fried tortillas with beans and sauce
Serves 4

Another antojito that is easy and quick to prepare. This is a combination of tortillas, beans and sauce, garnished with a little Spanish chorizo sausage (available from delicatessen counters). The quantities below are enough for a light lunch or supper.

4 fl oz (110 ml) cooking oil
8 corn tortillas or 4 wheat flour tortillas
1¼ lb (500 g) Frijoles Refritos (recipe on p. 20)
½ pt (300 ml) Salsa de Jitomate (recipe on p. 24)
4 oz (100 g) crumbly white cheese, such as Wensleydale
1 onion, chopped finely
2 green chillies, chopped finely
8 oz (225 g) Spanish chorizo or other spicy sausage, crumbled, fried
  and drained

Heat the oil in a frying pan and toss each tortilla in it for 1 minute, turning once and removing from the oil when just light brown. Drain the tortillas on absorbent paper and keep them warm.

Spread each tortilla with the hot re-fried beans and 2 tablespoons (2 × 15 ml spoon) of the cooked tomato sauce and then sprinkle it with some of the cheese, onions, chorizo and chillies. Serve immediately.

Chilaquiles

Crispy fried corn tortillas in tomato sauce
Serves 4

These go very well with Frijoles Refritos (recipe on p. 20) and
are a traditional breakfast dish which is good enough for
lunch or light supper. Excellent in an emergency if you have
some tortillas in the freezer.

oil for deep frying
12 corn tortillas, cut into 8 pieces each
1 pint (600 ml) Salsa de Jitomate (recipe on p. 24)
1 medium-size onion, chopped finely

Optional extras
2 green chillies, chopped finely
4 tablespoons (4 × 15 ml spoon) soured cream
2 oz (50 g) Wensleydale cheese, crumbled

Heat the oil to 400°F/200°C and fry the tortillas until they
start changing colour. Drain them and keep them warm.

Bring the sauce to the boil, drop the tortilla chips into it and
bring to the boil again. Transfer the mixture to a warm
serving dish and garnish it with the chopped onion and the
chillies if used. Add the soured cream and cheese before
garnishing if you wish to turn it into a lunch or supper dish.

Enfrijoladas and Chilaquiles

Huevos con Tortilla

Tortilla omelette
Serves 4

A quick and tasty way of eating eggs, this would make a popular light supper or brunch.

3 fried tortillas, quartered into bite-sized pieces
4 tablespoons (4 × 15 ml spoon) cooking oil, plus more for deep frying
½ onion, chopped
4 large eggs (size 2), lightly beaten and mixed with 1 teaspoon (5 ml spoon) water
6 sprigs of parsley, chopped finely
2 green chillies (optional)
a pinch of salt
a pinch of ground black pepper
6 tablespoons (6 × 15 ml spoon) Salsa de Jitomate (recipe on p. 24)

Fry the tortilla pieces in a deep fat fryer until golden brown, about 3 minutes.

Heat the 4 tablespoons (4 × 15 ml spoon) oil in a frying pan, and sauté the onion. Add the beaten egg, parsley, chillies if used, tortilla pieces, salt and pepper. Stir slowly, moving the egg mixture to one side and tilting the frying pan to ensure that all the egg gets cooked.

In order to cook the egg mixture on the other side, transfer it from the frying pan on to a dinner plate. Now place the frying pan upside down over the plate. Holding both the plate and the frying pan with oven gloves, turn them over so that the plate is uppermost. Remove the plate and return the frying pan to the heat for 1 more minute. (All this extra trouble should produce a rounded omelette about 1 inch/2.5 cm thick.) Spread the hot tomato sauce over it and serve hot, accompanied by Frijoles Refritos (p. 20).

Bocadillos y Entremeses

Hors d'oeuvres and starters

Meals in Mexico are at no set time, so that bocadillos are very necessary as well as popular, especially for celebrations. You might be invited at two o'clock for lunch and the meal may not actually start until four o'clock. But the bocadillos, accompanied by tequila, mezcal or beer will, in fact, provide delicious hors d'oeuvres before the meal properly begins.

Meal time in Mexico is a happy time, time to relax and to socialise as well as to satisfy your appetite. The influence of Spain and France in Mexican cuisine is very evident and the delightful mixture that results is pleasing to both eye and palate. Olives are often offered by themselves, and anchovies and smoked oysters on crackers are also popular, as are peanuts tossed in a healthy helping of cayenne pepper. I have included in this section some recipes for the most popular bocadillos, bearing in mind the availability of ingredients in Britain.

Sopa, soup, is a dish acquired from colonial times, and despite the heat in the middle of the day no meal is complete without it. It is served hot throughout the year. A good *caldo*, or stock, is of utmost importance, and the basic Mexican stock (p. 47) is well worth making in quantity to give extra flavour to the soup recipes on the following pages. Ingredients such as beans, avocado pears, pumpkin blossoms, stale tortillas and fresh and dried chillies provide a great diversity of flavours.

More unusual is the second soup, called *sopa seca*, 'dry soup', which is also generally served before the meat course. These 'soups' usually consist of rice or pasta cooked in tomato sauce and stock (which is absorbed in the cooking) and finally sprinkled with cheese.

Cebiche

Marinated fish
Serves 8 as a starter or 4 as a lunch

Cebiche is the traditional dish of the coastal towns, where it takes many different guises, the ingredients being as varied as the people that prepare it. Red snapper is the most popular fish used, but cod and haddock can be used instead. Whatever your views on eating raw fish, do try it!

1 lb (450 g) cod or haddock fillets, skinned
1 medium-size onion, sliced finely
juice of 1 orange
juice of 5 limes or lemons
4 tablespoons (4 × 15 ml spoon) olive oil
3 tablespoons (3 × 15 ml spoon) tomato ketchup
1 teaspoon (5 ml spoon) Worcestershire sauce
½ teaspoon (2.5 ml spoon) oregano
½ teaspoon (2.5 ml spoon) salt
¼ teaspoon (1.25 ml spoon) ground black pepper
½ pint (300 ml) Salcita de Jitomate (recipe on p. 23)
avocado slices, to garnish (optional)

Inspect the fish carefully for bones and remove them. Cut the fillets into small, bite-size pieces and place in a bowl with the sliced onion and the fresh orange and lime or lemon juice, taking care that all the fish is well covered. Cover and leave in the refrigerator to marinate overnight, or for at least 3 hours.

An hour before serving, add the remaining ingredients, stir and then leave to marinate until required. The fish will have 'cooked' in the acidic fruit juice and should be white, not transparent. Serve cold, garnished if desired with avocado slices and accompanied by water biscuits.

Cebiche, Salpicón de Hongos and Jaiba al Horno served in scallop shells

Jaiba al Horno

Baked crab
Serves 4

This dish is excellent with either fresh or canned crab. If you use whole crabs, scrub and save the crab shells, as they can be used to bake the crab in.

In Mexico City it is possible to go to the fish market and buy live crabs. In fact the market proudly proclaims in huge letters 'The fish that you buy here today slept in the sea last night.' The variety of fish and seafood available is incredible.

2 oz (50 g) butter or margarine
1 medium-size onion, chopped finely
5 sprigs of fresh parsley, chopped finely
6 oz (175 g) white crab meat, fresh, canned or frozen
2 dashes of Tabasco sauce
¼ teaspoon (1.25 ml spoon) Worcestershire sauce
½ chicken stock cube
a pinch of ground black pepper
3 tablespoons (3 × 15 ml spoon) tomato purée
2 tablespoons (2 × 15 ml spoon) fine breadcrumbs
4 slices of lemon, to garnish

Melt the butter in a heavy frying pan and sauté the onions and parsley for 2 minutes. Drain the crab meat well and add it to the pan, along with all the other ingredients except for the breadcrumbs and lemon. Fry over moderate heat, stirring frequently, until the mixture starts to dry.

Spoon on to well-buttered scallop or crab shells and bake at Gas Mark 4/350°F/180°C. After 15 minutes sprinkle the breadcrumbs on top and return to the oven; when the breadcrumbs are lightly browned it is ready. Serve hot, garnished with lemon slices.

Salpicón de Hongos

Marinated mushrooms
Serves 4

A quick and easy dish to be used as a cold starter or as a hot filling for soft, warm tortillas. Ideal for vegetarians.

2 tablespoons (2 × 15 ml spoon) cooking oil
1 clove of garlic
8 oz (225 g) mushrooms, sliced coarsely
1 medium-size onion, sliced
1 carrot, grated finely
2 sticks of celery, sliced crossways
1 green pepper, sliced
1 chilli, chopped finely
juice of ½ lime or lemon
1 chicken stock cube or a pinch of salt (optional)
a pinch of sugar
a pinch of ground black pepper
6 sprigs of fresh coriander, chopped finely
4 oz (100 g) full fat soft cheese (optional)

Heat the oil in a heavy skillet and sauté the garlic clove until dark golden. Discard the garlic clove, then sauté the mushrooms, onion, carrot, celery, pepper and chilli for 5 minutes. Add the lime juice, crumbled stock cube, sugar, black ground pepper and coriander. Cover and simmer for a further 5 minutes. Serve cold.

To serve hot, add the soft cheese and use as filling for tortillas.

Totopos

Tortilla chips
Serves 4

Everyone loves tortilla chips, and they are an excellent alternative to crisps. You can make them well in advance since they will keep in an airtight container for up to a week.

6–8 tortillas
oil for deep frying
2 teaspoons (2 × 5 ml spoon) salt
4 tablespoons (4 × 15 ml spoon) parmesan cheese (optional)
½ teaspoon (2.5 ml spoon) cayenne pepper (optional)

Cut the tortillas into quarters and then cut each quarter in half to form eight triangles. Alternatively, corn tortillas can be cut into strips, 2 × ½ inches (4 × 1 cm), but this is not advisable for wheat flour tortillas, which break too easily.

Heat the oil to the same temperature as for frying chips, about 400°F/200°C. Fry the pieces until they are light brown, stirring them occasionally and making sure all the tortillas brown evenly. Drain them on absorbent paper and toss with salt and parmesan and/or cayenne if required. Serve cold, alone or with a dip such as Guacamole (recipe on p. 25) or the next recipe, Frijoles con Queso. These chips also make a good garnish for Frijoles Refritos (p. 20).

Guacamole with Totopos and Cacahuates Enchilados make good hors d'oeuvres served with Margarita cocktails (see Drinks section)

Frijoles con Queso
Bean and cheese dip
Serves 6

This is a good cocktail snack, served warm with Totopos (see preceding recipe).

½ lb (225 g) Frijoles Refritos (recipe on p. 20)
2 oz (50 g) mild Cheddar cheese, grated finely
½ pint (323 ml) Salcita de Jitomate (recipe on p. 23)

Warm the re-fried beans if necessary; they should be the consistency of thick porridge. Add the grated cheese and stir for about 1 minute until the cheese melts. Remove from the heat and mix in the tomato sauce. Allow to cool to room temperature and serve with Totopos. (Stir just before serving if made in advance.)

Cacahuates Enchilados
Peppered peanuts
Serves 4

Peanuts are eaten in Mexico in many different ways: plain, roasted, peppered, sugared and also ground into sauces. This is one popular way of serving them.

7 oz (200 g) packet of roasted peanuts
1 teaspoon (5 ml spoon) cayenne pepper

Mix the peanuts thoroughly with the pepper. Offer in bowls with drinks.

Caldo de Pollo

Mexican-style chicken stock
Makes 2 pints (1.2 litres)

Caldo de Pollo is a must for Mexican soups. It is economical because it utilises the goodness in the carcass, leaving the flesh for use in other dishes. The recipe is also suitable for beef or lamb bones. This stock can be served as consommé – garnish with fresh lime. It will then serve six.

a 3 lb (1.35 kg) fresh chicken, preferably with the giblets
1 scant teaspoon (5 ml spoon) salt
¼ teaspoon (1.25 ml spoon) ground black pepper
3 tablespoons (3 × 15 ml spoon) malt vinegar
4 pints (2.4 litres) water
1 chicken stock cube
2 sticks of celery, chopped
2 medium-size carrots, chopped
3 cabbage leaves, shredded
6 sprigs of fresh coriander or parsley
3 cloves of garlic
3 medium-size onions, chopped

Wash the chicken well, inside and out. Remove the 'parson's nose' and any yellow skin on the giblets.

Put the chicken in a large saucepan with all the other ingredients. Cover and simmer at boiling point for 1 hour. Skim off any foam that comes to the surface. Test the chicken for readiness by pricking the drumstick. If only white liquid comes out and the leg feels loose, the chicken is ready.

Remove the chicken, strain the vegetables and taste the stock; if the flavour is weak, add one more stock cube and boil for a further 5 minutes. Skim off all the grease. This is done more successfully after the stock has been refrigerated for 2 hours.

The cold chicken meat can be used in other dishes, such as Tostadas (p. 32), Budin Azteca (p. 66) or Tacos (p. 71).

Sopa de Fideo

Vermicelli soup
Serves 4

This is an everyday soup in the Mexican home and is served 'dry', sprinkled with parmesan cheese and/or chopped fresh parsley. This dish improves if left overnight.

6 tablespoons (6 × 15 ml spoon) cooking oil
4 oz (100 g) vermicelli
½ onion, quartered
1 clove of garlic, skewered on a cocktail stick
4 sprigs of parsley
2 whole chillies
2 pints (1.2 litres) Caldo de Pollo (preceding recipe) or 3 chicken stock cubes dissolved in 2 pints (1.2 litres) boiling water
3 tablespoons (3 × 15 ml spoon) tomato purée

To garnish
2 oz (50 g) parmesan cheese
1 tablespoon (15 ml spoon) chopped parsley

Heat the oil in a large frying pan and fry the vermicelli until it is golden brown – this happens very quickly. Remove the vermicelli with a slotted spoon and drain on absorbent paper.

Discard all but 2 tablespoons (2 × 15 ml spoon) of the oil and fry the onion and garlic until golden. Add the reserved vermicelli, parsley, chillies, stock and tomato purée and stir so that the purée is well mixed in.

Cover and simmer for 15 minutes; then uncover and cook for a further 30 minutes, stirring occasionally. When the mixture starts to dry out, it is ready to serve. Discard the onion, garlic, parsley and chillies and serve sprinkled with the parmesan cheese and chopped parsley or keep to reheat the next day.

A selection of Mexican soups: Sopa de Poro y Papa, Sopa de Aguacate and a 'dry soup', Sopa de Fideo

Sopa de Poro y Papa

Leek and potato soup
Serves 4

A simple and delicious soup. Eat it hot as it is, or cold by
adding double cream and putting it in the blender.

2 pints (1.2 litres) Caldo de Pollo (recipe on p. 47) or 3 chicken stock
    cubes dissolved in 2 pints (1.2 litres) boiling water
2 fresh leeks, sliced thinly
2 medium-size potatoes, peeled and cubed
2 tablespoons (2 × 15 ml spoon) fresh parsley or coriander, chopped
    finely
a pinch of sugar
salt and ground black pepper
5 fl oz (150 ml) double cream (for cold soup only)

Bring the stock to the boil. Add the leek and potato and
simmer until tender. Add all the other ingredients and
simmer for 20 minutes more. Serve hot.

For cold soup, allow to cool, and then add the double
cream. Mix in a blender and serve garnished with more
coriander or parsley.

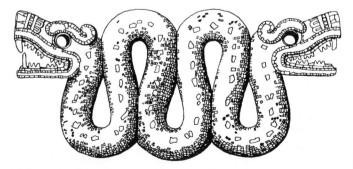

Sopa de Frijol Negro

Black bean soup
Serves 8

This is a delicious, hearty soup, as well as an excellent way of finishing leftover beans. It can actually be cooked with any type of bean, as the colour is unimportant and flavour varies only slightly. Black beans themselves, which are rich in iron and protein, have a slightly mushroomy flavour and lend the soup a distinctive colour. The crôutons are the perfect complement to this soup, but can also be used as a garnish for many other soups or even added to tossed green salads.

6 tablespoons (6 × 15 ml spoon) cooking oil
1 pint (600 ml) Frijoles (half the recipe on p. 18) and their liquid, if any
2 tablespoons (2 × 15 ml spoon) tomato purée
½ onion
1 small clove of garlic
2 pints (1.2 litres) Caldo de Pollo (recipe on p. 47) or 3 chicken stock cubes dissolved in 2 pints (1.2 litres) boiling water
2 green chillies (optional)
8 sprigs of fresh coriander
a pinch of sugar
salt and black pepper
2 slices of stale white bread cut into ½-inch (1 cm) cubes

Heat 2 tablespoons (2 × 15 ml spoon) of the oil in a saucepan. Grind the beans, tomato purée, onion and garlic in a blender to a smooth paste, adding a little chicken stock if the mixture is too dry to blend.

Strain (or just pour) the mixture into the hot oil slowly to prevent it from splashing. Add the chicken stock, chillies, coriander, sugar and seasoning. Bring to the boil and simmer uncovered for 30 minutes, until thick. Discard the herbs and chillies; if you prefer it hot, chop the chillies finely and put them back in the soup.

In a frying pan, heat the remaining oil and fry the bread cubes until golden brown, stirring continually, and then drain them on absorbent kitchen paper. (Alternatively, you can bake them in the oven at Gas Mark 1/275°F/140°C for 30 minutes, turning them occasionally.) Serve the soup in warm bowls garnished with the croûtons.

Sopa de Aguacate
Avocado soup
Serves 8

This soup is delicious at room temperature. It has a beautiful colour, which the flavour lives up to completely.

2 pints (1.2 litres) Caldo de Pollo (recipe on p. 47) or 3 chicken stock
    cubes dissolved in 2 pints (1.2 litres) boiling water
4 avocado pears, peeled
2 tablespoons (2 × 15 ml spoon) chopped fresh coriander, to garnish

Reheat the stock if not using it freshly made and pour it into a blender. Add three of the avocado pears and blend at top speed for 30 seconds. Allow to cool to room temperature. Slice the remaining avocado and garnish the soup with the slices and with the coriander sprinkled over the top.

Platos Fuertes
Main courses and accompaniments

When the European olives, oil, garlic, coriander and onions were added to native corn, tomatoes, chillies and courgettes, the possible combinations for Mexican main meals with fish, meat and poultry became endless.

Mexico's coastline stretches over 6,000 miles and provides a great variety of shellfish as well as fresh fish. The cooking of all these has evolved from the simple steaming in *maguey* (agave) leaves to frying, grilling and stewing. It is said that Emperor Moctezuma ate fresh fish every day – it was delivered by relays of barefoot runners from the Gulf of Mexico to Tenochtitlan, the Aztec capital.

The turkey was found domesticated in Mexico in the sixteenth century. Chicken, introduced by Spain into the Americas, has for economic reasons established itself well in the Mexican cuisine, but the most traditional dish is still made with turkey and is called *Mole de Guajolote* (*mole* is a traditionally spicy chilli sauce).

Pork, beef, lamb and goat were all unknown to the Indians until the Spaniards arrived. Pork in particular became very popular, as it yielded fat for cooking – the indigenous diet had been practically fatless. Beef and its by-products are expensive in Mexico, since pasture land is at a premium. The cheaper cuts of beef are often tough, hence its preparation in the form of stews and minced or shredded beef. Lamb is only popular in the form of *barbacoa*. This involves a primitive way of cooking the complete animal in a hole in the ground.

Because of Mexico's variety of climates and altitudes, practically any vegetable can be grown successfully somewhere in the Mexican Republic. It is a vegetarian's paradise, since apart from most of the European vegetables, which can be found all year round, there is a wealth of regional seasonal ones, which cooked in their traditional manner often become succulent main courses.

Torta de Pescado

Pilchard and potato casserole
Serves 6

A good, nourishing, tasty and economical dish. Freshly
cooked fish or canned tuna or salmon may be used instead of
canned pilchards, but some tomato purée must then be
added.

1 lb (450 g) potatoes
2 oz (50 g) margarine
1 chicken stock cube
¼ teaspoon (1.25 ml spoon) salt
a pinch of ground black pepper
15 oz (425 g) can of pilchards in tomato sauce or 2 × 7 oz (198 g) cans
    of salmon or tuna with 3 tablespoons (3 × 15 ml spoon) tomato
    purée
2 small eggs (size 4)
3 sprigs of fresh parsley, chopped, and extra sprigs to garnish
2 teaspoons (2 × 5 ml spoon) baking powder
¼ teaspoon (1.25 ml spoon) Worcestershire sauce

Peel and boil potatoes. When they are soft, drain and add the
margarine, stock cube, salt and pepper and mash the potatoes
whilst they are still hot. Cover them and keep them warm.

Cut the pilchards in half lengthways and remove all the
small bones. Add the eggs, parsley, baking powder and
Worcestershire sauce to the pilchards and mix well. Add this
to the potato mixture, mix and transfer to a well-greased
ovenproof dish.

Bake in a moderate oven, Gas Mark 4/350°F/180°C, for
30–40 minutes or until it browns on top. Garnish with fresh
parsley and serve hot with cooked vegetables or with sliced
tomatoes and a green salad.

Pescado a la Veracruzana

Fish in a tomato sauce
Serves 6

Veracruz is a very important port in the Gulf of Mexico and is the home of this traditional dish, a blend of Spanish and Mexican cuisine at its best. It is generally made with red snapper, which is found in the Gulf of Mexico and is considered a delicacy; haddock is similar in texture and is used in the recipe here. The capers and olives make it appetising and colourful, and it is an excellent main course for fish lovers.

2½ lb (1.1 kg) haddock fillets
1 lime or lemon, halved
½ teaspoon (2.5 ml spoon) salt
¼ teaspoon (1.25 ml spoon) ground black pepper
1½ pints (900 ml) Salsa de Jitomate (recipe on p. 24)
juice of 1 orange
2 red peppers, sliced finely with the seeds removed
1 large onion, sliced finely
18 stuffed olives
2 bay leaves
1 tablespoon (15 ml spoon) capers, drained
4 sprigs of fresh parsley
2 green chillies, whole or sliced finely (optional)
slices of orange and sprigs of parsley, to garnish

Wipe the fish and rub it all over with the lime or lemon. Season it with the salt and pepper. Spoon half of the Salsa into an ovenproof dish and place the fish on top. Add the orange juice, red pepper, onion, olives, bay leaves, capers, sprigs of parsley and chillies and pour the remaining sauce over it.

Cover with foil and bake in a moderate oven, Gas Mark 4/ 350°F/180°C, for 1 hour. To serve, rearrange the pepper slices and the olives so that they show and garnish with orange slices and sprigs of parsley. Serve with warm, crusty bread or rice and a green vegetable.

Camarones al Mojo de Ajo

Prawns in garlic
Serves 4

This dish is delicious and, despite the fact that in Mexico prawns are much bigger, small frozen prawns done in this manner are just as good. The garlic flavour is much milder than you would expect and may even pass unnoticed.

2 tablespoons (2 × 15 ml spoon) cooking oil
2 tablespoons (2 × 15 ml spoon) butter or margarine
2 cloves of garlic, chopped very finely
½ medium-size onion, chopped very finely
2 oz (50 g) fresh parsley, chopped finely, and extra sprigs for garnish
1 green chilli, chopped finely (optional)
1 lb (450 g) raw shelled prawns, fresh or thawed from frozen
½ chicken stock cube
a pinch of ground black pepper
juice of ½ lime or lemon, and slices for garnish

Heat the oil and butter in a large, heavy frying pan. Add the garlic, onion, chopped parsley and chilli, and fry until the parsley starts to look very dark green and dry.

Add the prawns, crushed stock cube, black pepper and lime or lemon juice. Increase the heat and stir-fry for 3 minutes. Serve individually, garnishing each portion with fresh parsley and slices of lime or lemon. Serve with Arroz Blanco (p. 60), Guacamole (p. 25) and a green salad.

Pescado a la Veracruzana and Camarones al Mojo de Ajo

Chiles Rellenos de Frijol

Peppers stuffed with beans
Serves 6

This dish is delicious and makes a good meatless main course
for summer. It must be prepared two days before it is needed,
as the peppers need to marinate.

4 fl oz (110 ml) olive or corn oil
6 medium-size green peppers, stalks and seeds removed
3 large onions, sliced thinly
1½ pints (900 ml) malt vinegar
1 tablespoon (15 ml spoon) sugar
2 green chillies, thinly sliced
2 teaspoons (2 × 5 ml spoon) oregano
1 teaspoon (5 ml spoon) thyme
1 teaspoon (5 ml spoon) cumin
2 bay leaves
½ teaspoon (2.5 ml spoon) salt
¼ teaspoon (1.25 ml spoon) ground black pepper
1¼ lb (500 g) Frijoles Refritos (recipe on p. 20)

Heat the oil in a large, heavy frying pan and sauté the peppers
and onions until the onions turn translucent. Slowly add the
vinegar, sugar, chillies and all the spices and then simmer
until the peppers are soft. Remove the onions and peppers
from the liquid and continue simmering until it is reduced by
half.

In the meantime, allow the peppers to cool and remove any
blistered skin from them (it is not necessary to remove all the
skin). Stuff the peppers with the re-fried beans and secure the
tops with cocktail sticks if necessary.

Arrange the peppers in a serving dish, placing the onions
over them. Then pour the hot spiced vinegar over them.
When cool, leave them uncovered in the fridge or a cool place
for two days before serving. Try these peppers with Arroz
Blanco (p. 60), Guacamole (p. 25) and warm, soft tortillas.

Chiles en Nogada

Stuffed peppers in walnut sauce
Serves 8

It is traditional to eat these peppers in early September when the walnuts are green and easy to peel. September is the patriotic month in Mexico and the green, white and red in this dish are said to have been planned to match the colours of the Mexican flag.

8 green peppers
12 oz (350 g) Picadillo (half the recipe on p. 22)
shredded lettuce
3 oz (75 g) walnuts, chopped finely
2 oz (50 g) ground almonds
4 oz (100 g) cream cheese
5 fl oz (150 ml) carton of single cream
1 teaspoon (5 ml spoon) lemon juice
¼ teaspoon (1.25 ml spoon) salt
pomegranate kernels (optional), to garnish
7 oz (200 g) can of red peppers, to garnish

Place the peppers on a hot grill, turning them round as the skins blister. Remove each pepper when it is ready and cover with a damp tea towel for 10–15 minutes. This helps to steam them and to flavour the flesh. Peel off any burnt skin you can. Cut off the stalks by cutting around them with a sharp knife and then remove the seeds. Stuff the peppers with 2 tablespoons (2 × 15 ml spoon) Picadillo. Close the opening and secure if necessary with a cocktail stick or two. If the pepper breaks anywhere else, hold it together with more cocktail sticks. Arrange the peppers on a bed of shredded lettuce.

Mix together the walnut pieces, ground almonds, cream cheese, cream, lemon juice and salt. Pour this mixture over the peppers and decorate with pomegranate kernels, if desired, and strips of canned red pepper. Serve cold with Arroz Blanco (see next recipe) and salad.

Arroz Blanco

Mexican-style white rice
Serves 6–8

Rice was introduced into Mexico by the Spanish and is now grown and eaten in Mexico regularly. When used as a main course, it is cooked with chicken, fish and vegetables. Otherwise it is treated as a side dish. This particular way of cooking rice is suitable for any recipe calling for plain rice and it's great! It's nice and fluffy, it doesn't stick and it's much tastier than plain boiled rice.

4 tablespoons (4 × 15 ml spoon) cooking oil
12 oz (350 g) long grain white rice
1½ pints (900 ml) hot water
½ teaspoon (2.5 ml) salt
1 chicken stock cube
2 sprigs of fresh coriander or parsley
1 medium-size onion, chopped finely
2 whole green chillies
1 clove of garlic, skewered on a cocktail stick

Heat the oil in a thick-bottomed pan which has a tight-fitting lid. Add the rice and sauté, stirring continually, for about 4 minutes or until the rice changes colour.

Drain off all the excess oil and then add the water and all the other ingredients. Cover and bring to the boil quickly. Now reduce the heat and simmer, covered, for 15 minutes or until all the water is absorbed; the rice should double in volume and become light and fluffy. Discard the garlic and the cocktail stick, herbs and chillies. Serve hot or cold.

To freeze, cool the rice and store it in an airtight container. To thaw, leave it at room temperature for about 1 hour. To reheat, place the rice in a pan with 2 tablespoons (2 × 15 ml spoon) of water in the bottom, cover and place over low heat or in a medium hot oven, Gas Mark 4/350°F/180°C, for about 20 minutes.

Chiles en Nogada and Arroz Blanco

To make a rice mould   Oil a ring mould and press the newly cooked rice gently but firmly into the mould whilst it is still warm. To serve the rice immediately, turn it upside down on a hot platter and fill the centre with Guacamole (recipe on p. 25) or Rajas Encebolladas (recipe on p. 64). To serve the rice later, cover the mould with kitchen foil and place it in a pan of water in a low oven, Gas Mark 2/300°F/150°C, for 30 minutes, then serve as above.

Arroz Poblano
Rice with cream, cheese and peppers
Serves 10

This dish is made in Mexico from local Poblano peppers, but the peppers you buy in Britain are an acceptable substitute. Although it is an excellent way to use up leftover Arroz Blanco, it is delicious enough to justify cooking some specially.

1 quantity of Arroz Blanco (preceding recipe)
1 red and 1 green pepper, halved, deseeded and cut into strips
5 fl oz (150 ml) carton of soured cream, diluted with 4 tablespoons (4 × 15 ml spoon) milk
4 oz (100 g) mild Cheddar cheese, grated finely

Lightly grease a rectangular ovenproof dish, and fill with layers of the cooked rice, pepper strips, soured cream and grated cheese. Repeat in that order, finishing with the cheese on top. Bake on the top shelf of a moderate oven, Gas Mark 4/350°F/180°C, for 35 minutes or until the cheese browns. Serve hot.

Enchiladas

Rolled tortillas in tomato sauce
Serves 6

A very popular and traditional dish and very versatile, too. Enchiladas have a filling of chopped raw onions and crumbly white cheese. However, they can be filled with shredded or minced cooked meat or scrambled eggs. The sauces also vary, tomato sauce being the most popular and the easiest to make in Britain. For Enchiladas the tortillas must always be sealed in hot oil first, to prevent them from absorbing too much liquid and becoming mushy. Allow about three small (corn) or two large (wheat flour) tortillas per person. Enchiladas should be eaten hot, immediately after preparation, so this dish is not advisable for large numbers.

18 corn or 12 wheat flour tortillas
8 fl oz (225 ml) cooking oil
1½ pints (900 ml) Salsa de Jitomate (recipe on p. 24)
8 oz (225 g) crumbly white cheese such as Wensleydale
2 medium-size onions, chopped finely

Alternative fillings
4 eggs, scrambled, *or* 1 whole chicken breast, cooked and shredded

Shallow-fry each tortilla in very hot oil for 30 seconds. Drain on absorbent kitchen paper and keep warm until all the tortillas are fried.

Bring the Salsa de Jitomate to boiling point and then keep it on low heat (if it thickens too much add a little water). To make the first serving, dip one tortilla in the sauce, remove and put it on a warm plate; repeat for two more tortillas. Sprinkle the centre of each of these tortillas with cheese (or one of the alternative fillings) and onion, and roll it up. When all three tortillas have been rolled, spoon more sauce over them and sprinkle with more of the chosen filling and onion. Serve immediately with Frijoles Refritos (recipe on p. 20) and green salad or Rajas Encebolladas (see next recipe). Repeat the procedure for the remaining servings.

Rajas Encebolladas

Peppers with onion rings
Serves 6

This is a colourful and tasty side dish, good with Enchiladas,
Carnitas (p. 79) and many other dishes. It can be turned into a
main dish with the addition of leftover roast pork.

2 tablespoons (2 × 15 ml spoon) cooking oil
2 large onions, sliced thinly
4 green peppers, cut into strips
4 green chillies, sliced thinly (optional)
3 tablespoons (3 × 15 ml spoon) tomato purée
1 chicken stock cube
¼ teaspoon (1.25 ml spoon) salt
a pinch of ground black pepper
a pinch of sugar
4 sprigs of fresh coriander (optional)
6 fl oz (175 ml) water
½ Camembert cheese, sliced thinly, or 4 oz (100 g) mild Cheddar,
    grated finely
5 fl oz (150 ml) carton of soured cream

Heat the oil in a heavy frying pan, add the onions and sauté
them until they are soft. Remove the onions and then sauté
the peppers until soft. Replace the onions and add the
chillies, if used, the tomato purée, crumbled stock cube, salt,
pepper, sugar and coriander if available. Add the water, stir
and cover. Simmer gently for 5 minutes and then mix in the
cheese and cream. Transfer the mixture to an ovenproof dish
and bake at Gas Mark 4/350°F/180°C for 15 minutes or until
the cheese melts.

Variation To make this into a main-course dish in its own
right, add 8 oz (225 g) cold roast pork with the cheese and
cream before baking. Serve wrapped in soft, warm tortillas.

Enchiladas, served with garnished Frijoles Refritos and Rajas Encebolladas

Budin Azteca

Chicken tortilla casserole
Serves 8–10

This easy dish, also known as Moctezuma Pie, is designed to cope with large numbers. It's ideal for a buffet and easy to prepare ahead of time, but remember to save some sauce to pour over it just before serving. The tortillas should be done ahead of time.

18 corn or 12 wheat flour tortillas
8 fl oz (225 ml) corn oil
1½ pints (900 ml) Salsa de Jitomate (recipe on p. 24)
a 3 lb (1.35 kg) chicken, boiled, skinned and boned
2 green peppers, sliced
½ pint (300 ml) soured cream
1 onion, chopped finely
8 oz (225 g) mild Cheddar cheese, grated finely

Shallow-fry the tortillas in very hot oil for about 30 seconds on each side. Drain them on absorbent kitchen paper and keep them warm until they are all fried.

Bring the Salsa de Jitomate to the boil. Pour 4 tablespoons (4 × 15 ml spoon) over the bottom of a 12-inch (30 cm) diameter ovenproof dish. Dip a third of the tortillas, one at a time, in the hot sauce and lay them on the bottom of the casserole. Overlap the tortillas so that all are lying flat. Spoon some more of the sauce over the tortillas to cover them, making sure all the edges are well soaked.

Arrange about a third of the chicken pieces on top, followed by peppers, soured cream and chopped onion; then sprinkle liberally with grated cheese. Repeat twice, until all the tortillas are used, finishing with soured cream and cheese. If you are using flour tortillas, it is preferable to use only three tortillas per layer and have more layers.

Bake uncovered in a moderate oven, Gas Mark 4/350°F/180°C, for 40 minutes and serve hot, accompanied with Frijoles Refritos (recipe on p. 20), courgettes, a corn or green salad and slices of avocado.

Chilli con Carne

Spicy meat casserole
Serves 10

Chilli con Carne is not really a Mexican dish. Its origins are in Mexico, though, and in all probability it was when the Americans came over the border for Mexican food and were offered the spicy meat dish Mole de Guajolote, accompanied by fried beans and white rice, that they were inspired to try something similar when they went back home. I have included this well-known recipe instead of Mole de Guajolote, as the latter requires a number of ingredients not easily found in this country. Although American Chilli con Carne is generally made with minced beef, cubed pork is more commonly used in Mexico for dishes of this type, as here.

2½ lb (1.7 kg) shoulder of pork, cubed
2 tablespoons (2 × 15 ml spoon) malt vinegar
½ teaspoon (2.5 ml spoon) salt
¼ teaspoon (1.25 ml spoon) black pepper
a pinch of sugar
8 tablespoons (8 × 15 ml spoon) cooking oil
2 bay leaves
2 pints (1.2 litres) water
2 pints (1.2 litres) Frijoles (recipe on p. 18)
2 cloves of garlic
2 onions
4 green chillies (fewer for a milder dish)
6 sprigs of fresh coriander
1 teaspoon (5 ml spoon) powdered cinnamon, or a 2-inch (5 cm)
    piece of cinnamon stick
10 cloves
½ teaspoon (2.5 ml spoon) oregano
½ teaspoon (2.5 ml spoon) marjoram
1 teaspoon (5 ml spoon) sesame seed
6 tablespoons (6 × 15 ml spoon) chilli powder (less for a milder dish)
2 teaspoons (2 × 5 ml spoon) cayenne pepper (less for a milder dish)
6 tablespoons (6 × 15 ml spoon) tomato purée
14 oz (397 g) can of peeled tomatoes, well mashed

Season the meat with the vinegar, salt, pepper and sugar and leave it to marinate for 20 minutes.

Heat the oil and when it is very hot lightly fry the meat in it. Remove the meat and simmer it with the bay leaves in the water, until tender.

Meanwhile, put 5 fl oz (150 ml) of liquid from the cooked beans, the garlic, onion, chillies, herbs and spices together in a blender and liquidise. Fry the mixture in the remaining oil for about 2 minutes, stirring constantly. Strain the meat, reserving the liquid, and add it to the mixture together with the tomato purée, mashed tomatoes and cooked beans; simmer gently, stirring occasionally so that it does not stick.

In a separate pot, boil the reserved liquid from the meat until reduced by half, skimming off any foam. Add this to the mixture and simmer for about 15 minutes, to a thick consistency. Serve with Arroz Blanco (p. 60), a tossed green salad and warm tortillas. This dish freezes well and can be refrigerated for up to three days.

Salpicón

Shredded cold beef salad
Serves 4

A popular name given to this dish is *Ropa Vieja* ('tatty clothes').

1 lb (450 g) cold roast beef, shredded
½ pint (300 ml) Salcita de Jitomate (recipe on p. 23)
onion rings and slices of lime or lemon, to garnish

Mix the shredded cooked beef with the Salcita, garnish and serve cold with Arroz Blanco (p. 60), a tossed green salad and warm, soft tortillas. You place some of the meat in the centre of a tortilla, roll it up and eat it with the other accompaniments.

Totopo Salad and Salpicón

Totopo Salad

Green salad with crispy fried tortilla chips
Serves 4

This is a good salad for a light lunch and a good way to use up leftovers the day after the party!

1 lettuce, shredded finely
½ onion, chopped finely
2 tomatoes, chopped finely
6 sprigs of fresh coriander, chopped finely, plus whole sprigs to garnish
2 green chillies, chopped finely (optional)
8 oz (225 g) cooked chicken, turkey or beef, or shredded canned tuna fish
juice of 1 lime or lemon
½ teaspoon (2.5 ml spoon) salt
pinch of freshly ground black pepper
8 tortillas, cut into small squares and deep-fried (see Totopos recipe on p. 44)
1 ripe avocado

Mix together all the ingredients except the Totopos and the avocado half an hour before required. Just before serving, add the crisp Totopos and toss lightly. Cut the avocado into wedges and use it and the coriander sprigs as a garnish.

Taco Shells

Fried tortilla shells (pictured on the front cover)
Serves 4

Taco Shells are actually the American adaptation of the Mexican fried Tacos, which are tortillas with a filling rolled into a cigar shape and shallow-fried. Taco Shells are tortillas that are deep-fried in the shape of a horseshoe. This is a very practical shape, especially when you are entertaining large numbers: the filling is put on them after frying. Fresh or frozen tortillas may be used and they can be fried ahead of time. If they are going to be stored for more than an hour, however, it is preferable to let them cool and then keep them in an airtight container.

oil for deep frying
8 corn tortillas
1 lettuce, chopped finely
2 cooked chicken breasts, shredded finely
¼ pint (150 ml) Guacamole (recipe on p. 25)

Heat the oil (at least 4 inches/10 cm deep) in a deep fryer to 400°F/200°C as for chips. Immerse and fry the tortillas two at a time, holding them with kitchen tongs against the side of the fryer so as to resemble a horseshoe. After 1½–2 minutes they will have shaped and you can let go, separate them and turn them to ensure even frying. When they are light brown, drain on absorbent paper until required.

Fill with a combination of chopped lettuce, shredded chicken and 1 tablespoon (15 ml spoon) Guacamole. Other possible fillings are Picadillo (p. 22) with chopped lettuce and grated cheese, or Frijoles Refritos (p. 20) and Rajas Encebolladas (p. 64).

Variations   For cocktail parties, tortillas can be cut into 2½-inch (8 cm) circles with a biscuit cutter and then fried and filled in the same way. The cuttings needn't be wasted either, as they can be made into Totopos (see p. 44).

Chiles Rellenos

Stuffed peppers
Serves 6

Famous and very traditional, Chiles Rellenos is a hearty main dish. The peppers are filled with either spicy minced beef or cheese, and some of each type are often served at the same meal to give a choice of fillings. In Mexico Poblano peppers are used; they are a darker green and hotter than the capsicums sold in Britain. In order to make the peppers hotter I add green chillies to the sauce. The egg coating method is called *capear* and is also popular for parboiled cauliflower, broccoli and large courgettes.

6 medium-size green peppers
8 oz (225 g) mild Cheddar cheese or 1 lb (450 g) Picadillo (recipe on p. 22)
3 large eggs (size 1–2), separated
8 fl oz (225 ml) cooking oil
8 oz (225 g) plain flour
1½ pints (900 ml) Salsa de Jitomate (recipe on p. 24)

Place the peppers on a hot grill, turning them around as the skins blister. Remove each pepper when it is ready and cover with a damp tea towel for 10–15 minutes. This helps to steam them and to flavour the flesh.

Peel off any burnt skin you can. Cut off the stalks by cutting around them with a sharp knife, then remove the pips. Stuff the peppers with a slice of cheese or 2 tablespoons (2 × 15 ml spoon) Picadillo. Hold the opening together and secure it with a cocktail stick or two. If the pepper breaks anywhere else, hold it together with more cocktail sticks.

Beat the egg whites until they are stiff and beat the yolks until they change colour to a light yellow. Combine the two by stirring the yolk into the white gently.

Heat the oil in a frying pan. Toss each pepper in the flour,

Chiles Rellenos

and then dip it into the egg batter and carefully place it in the hot oil. Keep the heat low, as it will burn easily. Until you get more practice, fry only one at a time. Using a kitchen fork and spoon, turn the pepper around until it is golden brown all over. Remove it from the oil and drain on absorbent kitchen paper. Continue until all the peppers are fried.

Put 4 tablespoons (4 × 15 ml spoon) of the tomato sauce in an ovenproof dish and place the fried peppers in it. Pour the rest of the sauce over the peppers and cover the dish with aluminium foil. Bake at Gas Mark 4/350°F/180°C for about 1 hour. Serve hot, accompanied perhaps by warm, soft tortillas, Guacamole (p. 25) and Frijoles Refritos (p. 20).

Empanadas
Savoury turnovers
Serves 6

Empanadas are another good example of the influence of Spain on Mexican cuisine. They are popular throughout Latin America; the name is the same everywhere, but the fillings vary from savoury to sweet.

6 oz (175 g) self-raising flour
a pinch of salt
2 oz (50 g) margarine, cubed
2 oz (50 g) lard, cubed
½ teaspoon (2.5 ml spoon) fresh lime or lemon juice
3 fl oz (80 ml) cold water

For the filling
12 oz (350 g) Picadillo (half the recipe on p. 22)

Sift the flour and salt together and toss the fats in the flour until well coated. Using a spatula, mix the lime or lemon juice and water into the flour without breaking the lumps. Now add just enough extra liquid to bind the ingredients into a soft dough.

With floured fingers, form the dough into a soft ball, place on a well-floured board and shape it into a rectangle about 1 inch (2.5 cm) thick. With a floured rolling pin and short strokes, roll out the dough to a rectangle about ½ inch (1 cm) thick.

With a knife, lightly mark two horizontal lines, dividing the dough into three equal parts. Fold the lower third up over the centre and the top third down over the other two, trapping as much air as possible. Seal the sides together by pressing down firmly with the rolling pin. Repeat the rolling and folding three more times, turning the dough a quarter turn each time. Wrap in a polythene bag and chill for at least 1 hour. While it is chilling, prepare the Picadillo, or your own choice of filling, and allow it to cool.

Heat the oven to Gas Mark 7/425°F/220°C. Roll the pastry to the thickness of a coin and cut to the desired size. A 6-inch (16 cm) saucer is the right size of cutter for main course Empanadas.

Place 3 tablespoons (3 × 15 ml spoon) filling in the centre of each circle; dampen the edges of the dough with water, fold over and seal together. Place on a baking tray, brush with egg or milk and prick once with a fork. Bake for about 15 minutes. When they are golden, cool on a wire rack or serve hot. (In Mexico they also shallow-fry them instead of baking but with the extra taste come the extra calories!) Try them accompanied by Esquites and Arroz con Jitomate (see following recipes).

Variation Using a teacup as a cutter and proportionally less filling you can make delightful party-size Empanadas.

Esquites

Fried sweetcorn
Serves 4

Fresh corn sliced off the cob is used in many Mexican homes to produce a variety of side dishes. This recipe is traditionally cooked with *epazote*, a herb widely available in Mexico; parsley is an acceptable substitute.

2 tablespoons (2 × 15 ml spoon) cooking oil
½ medium-size onion, chopped finely
1 green pepper, deseeded and cut in thin strips
4 tablespoons (4 × 15 ml spoon) chopped parsley
1 chilli, deseeded and chopped finely (optional)
12 oz (350 g) fresh or frozen sweetcorn
4 oz (100 g) fresh mushrooms, sliced
1 chicken stock cube
a pinch of ground black pepper

Heat the oil in a frying pan and sauté the onion, pepper, parsley and chilli, if used. Add the sweetcorn, mushroom and crumbled stock cube. Stir, cover and cook over medium heat for 5 minutes. Uncover and continue frying for 5 minutes more, stirring frequently. Serve hot, sprinkled with black pepper.

Empanadas with Esquites and Arroz de Jitomate

Arroz con Jitomate

Tomato rice
Serves 8

This rice is traditionally made with fresh ripe tomatoes which have been charred, peeled and mashed, but I prefer to use tomato purée for convenience.

4 tablespoons (4 × 15 ml spoon) cooking oil
1 clove of garlic
12 oz (350 g) long grain white rice
6 tablespoons (6 × 15 ml spoon) tomato purée
1 teaspoon (5 ml spoon) salt
2 chicken stock cubes
4 sprigs of fresh parsley or coriander
1 medium-size onion, chopped finely
2 green chillies
4 oz (100 g) fresh or frozen peas
4 oz (100 g) fresh or frozen corn kernels
4 oz (100 g) fresh or frozen diced carrots
1¾ pints (1 litre) hot water

Heat the oil in a heavy saucepan with a close-fitting lid and fry the garlic clove until it is dark golden. Add the rice and fry, stirring frequently, until it too is golden or has absorbed all the oil. Discard the garlic clove.

Add the tomato purée and stir for 1 minute; then add all the other ingredients and stir. Bring to the boil quickly and then lower the heat, stir and cover. Simmer for 30 minutes or until all the water has disappeared.

Variation   Omit the salt and reduce the amount of tomato purée to 4 tablespoons (4 × 15 ml spoon). For the peas, corn kernels and carrots substitute 8 fl oz (225 ml) cooked beans (see Frijoles recipe, p. 18) and 5 fl oz (150 ml) of the bean juice. The amount of water should be reduced to 1¼ pints (750 ml).

Carnitas

Marinated roast pork
Serves 6

Carnitas are a typical outdoor meal; they are also the typical take-away Sunday lunch dish and the restaurants selling them are very numerous. They are usually eaten wrapped in a warm soft tortilla with various sauces and accompaniments, such as those suggested at the end of this recipe.

1 onion, chopped
2 cloves of garlic
1 teaspoon (5 ml spoon) salt
½ teaspoon (2.5 ml spoon) ground black pepper
a pinch of sugar
4 tablespoons (4 × 15 ml spoon) malt vinegar
4 lb (1.8 kg) shoulder of pork cut into 4-inch (10 cm) pieces with all
    the extra fat removed
1 pint (600 ml) water
1 lb (450 g) lard, cut into cubes

Liquidise together the onion, garlic, salt, black pepper, sugar and vinegar in a blender for 40 seconds at high speed. Smooth this paste all over the meat and leave it to marinate overnight or for at least 2 hours.

When marinated, put the meat and marinade in a large casserole dish with the water and lard. Cover and place it in a medium-hot oven, Gas Mark 3/325°F/170°C, for about 2 hours, basting and turning occasionally. Uncover and cook for a further half hour, turning once, until the meat is golden brown all over.

Drain off the extra fat. Pour the concentrated gravy over the meat and serve hot on a serving dish. Each person can then help himself to a portion and roll it up in a warm tortilla. Serve with sauces like Salcita de Jitomate (p. 23) or Guacamole (p. 25) and accompaniments such as Arroz Blanco (p. 60), Rajas Encebolladas (p. 64) and Frijoles (p. 18).

Postres
Desserts

In Mexico the main courses are so filling that desserts do not feature heavily. Fresh tropical fruits are often all that is offered, frequently without cream. Water ices of different fruit juices, ice creams and light, sweet milk desserts are also greatly enjoyed. Crystallised pumpkin, sweet potato and *chilacayotl* (known in Britain as 'vegetable spaghetti') are some of the many sweets offered after a meal.

Pastelitos de Boda
Sugared shortbread biscuits ('Wedding cakes')
Makes 40–50 1-inch (2.5 cm) diameter biscuits

Pastelitos are traditional wedding sweetmeats and are often coated in icing sugar to match the whiteness of the bride's dress. Similar to shortbread biscuits, they really melt in the mouth and are easy to make.

8 oz (225 g) butter or margarine
2 oz (50 g) caster sugar
8 oz (225 g) plain flour
4 oz (100 g) cornflour
2 oz (50 g) icing sugar, sieved, or 1 teaspoon (5 ml spoon) powdered cinnamon mixed with 4 oz (100 g) caster sugar

Cream the butter with the caster sugar until white and shiny. Sieve the plain flour and cornflour together, then gradually work them into the creamed mixture with a wooden spoon. Knead until smooth.

Take about 1 heaped teaspoon (2 × 5 ml spoon) of the mixture at a time and roll it in the palm of your hand. Arrange the little balls on a greased baking tray and bake in a slow oven, Gas Mark 3/325°F/170°C, for 30–40 minutes until they are pale golden.

Dulce de Chocolate con Canela and Pastelitos de Boda (tossed in cinnamon and sugar)

Whilst the biscuits are still warm, toss them in the icing sugar or cinnamon and sugar and then leave to cool on a wire rack.

Dulce de Chocolate con Canela
Chocolate and cinnamon blancmange
Serves 4

Although chocolate is more popular in Mexico as a drink than as a dessert, this is still a dessert with a distinctly Mexican flavour. It is a simple blancmange-style sweet, served cold in Mexico but just as nice hot on a British winter's day. It takes only a few minutes to prepare, and is also very good with vanilla ice cream.

1 pint (600 ml) milk
6 oz (175 g) granulated sugar
2 oz (50 g) cornflour
2 oz (50 g) plain cocoa powder
1 teaspoon (5 ml spoon) powdered cinnamon
1 oz (25 g) chopped nuts (optional)

Put everything except the nuts into a blender and blend at top speed for 45 seconds. Pour the mixture into a saucepan over a low heat, stirring briskly with a wire whisk for about 4 minutes until it starts to thicken.

Before it comes to the boil, sieve into a pudding bowl as quickly as possible to remove any lumps. Garnish with chopped nuts if desired and serve hot or cold with or without ice cream.

Ensalada de Fruta Tropical

Tropical fruit salad (pictured on the back cover)
Serves 6

Cantaloupe melons, water-melon, plums, pineapple, guavas
and paw-paw are all very popular fruits in Mexico and are
eaten on their own with a little sugar. Few desserts, however,
are more appetising than a tropical fruit salad. In Mexico it is
always served refrigerated and is often garnished with chopped pecan nuts instead of cream. If any fruit in this recipe is
not available, you can either use larger quantities of any of the
others or substitute oranges, bananas, passion fruit or peeled
grapes. Other exotic possibilities are paw-paw and prickly
pear.

4 oz (100 g) fresh strawberries
½ cantaloupe or honeydew melon
½ lb (225 g) water-melon
1 mango
½ small fresh pineapple or 7 oz (198 g) can of pineapple chunks in
   syrup
14½ oz (400 g) can of guavas in syrup
juice and slivered rind of 1 lemon
6 oz (175 g) granulated sugar
5 fl oz (150 ml) water (omit if canned pineapple used)

Halve the strawberries and put in a heat-resistant bowl. Cut
the melon into the bowl, putting the pips and veins in a
saucepan. Discard the peel and seeds of the water-melon, and
cube the flesh into the bowl. Cut the mango as near to the
centre of the stone as possible on both sides and cube the flesh
into the bowl; extract any juice left in the skins, scraping with
a knife if neccessary, and add to the saucepan. Core the
pineapple if fresh and add the core to the saucepan, cubing
the flesh into the bowl; if canned pineapple is used, drain the
syrup into the saucepan and add the chunks to the bowl.
Drain the guava syrup into the pan likewise; cut the fruit into
four and mix with the other fruit in the bowl.

Add the lemon juice and rind, sugar and water (if necessary) to the saucepan. Dissolve the sugar over a gentle heat and then bring to the boil. Boil for 2 minutes and then pour the liquid over the fruit through a strainer. Allow the bowl to cool and then refrigerate.

Helado de Mango
Mango ice cream
Makes 4 pints (2.4 litres); serves 12

A very different, very colourful and flavoursome ice cream. It can be made with any fruit purée: mangoes are my favourite, but raspberries and strawberries are delicious, too. You have to begin this dish at least two days before it is needed.

14 oz (397 g) can of evaporated milk
5 oz (150 g) icing sugar
1 tablespoon (15 ml spoon) lemon juice
1½ pints (900 ml) mango or other fruit purée, chilled

Remove the label from the can of evaporated milk and place *unopened* in a deep saucepan. Cover with water to 3 inches (8 cm) above the can. Bring to the boil and simmer for 15 minutes. Allow the canned milk to cool for at least 2 hours and then refrigerate it, still unopened, for 24 hours. (Do *not* open the can while hot.)

The next day, empty the can of evaporated milk into a very cold bowl and whisk with an electric mixer at top speed for about 5 minutes, until it thickens into a cream and more than doubles in bulk. Add the sugar, lemon juice and chilled fruit purée and mix at the lowest speed just until the fruit is well mixed into the cream. Pour into a chilled container, seal and freeze for at least 12 hours. It is best thawed in the fridge for about half an hour before use.

Helado de Mango

Piña Virreynal

Viceroy pineapple
Serves 8

During the 300 years that Spain had Mexico under its domain the Viceroys lived in great opulence and enjoyed the best food the country had to offer. This dessert is the Mexican answer to the British trifle. Sweet, cool and with a nicy rummy flavour, it is good in summer. If you double the amounts, it is easy and colourful for a party. Preparation starts the day before.

14 oz (397 g) can of sweetened condensed milk
1 medium-size fresh pineapple or 1 lb 13 oz (822 g) can of pineapple chunks, drained
6 fl oz (175 ml) dark rum or tequila
3 oz (75 g) icing sugar
2 packets of sponge fingers (approx. 36 fingers in all)
5 fl oz (150 ml) carton of double cream, whipped
kernels of 1 pomegranate or 2 oz (50 g) sliced almonds, to garnish

Place the *unopened* can of sweetened condensed milk in a saucepan of cold water, bring to the boil and boil for 2 hours, topping up with boiling water if necessary. Remove from the water, cool and refrigerate, still unopened.

The next day, peel, core and cut the pineapple into bite-size pieces, if a fresh one is used. Put the pieces or chunks in a bowl and pour the rum or tequila and the sugar over them; leave to soak for half an hour. Line the sides and base of a dish, 8 × 8 × 2 inches (20 × 20 × 5 cm), with the sponge fingers, dipping them briefly in the pineapple mixture first. Halve them to line the sides. Spread the pineapple and juice evenly over the sponge fingers.

Open the chilled can of condensed milk and whip it with an electric mixer for 5 minutes, until it is light and fluffy. Add the whipped double cream and mix. Spread this mixture evenly over the pineapple. Garnish with pomegranate kernels or sliced almonds and refrigerate until needed.

Chongos Zamoranos

Curds in syrup
Serves 6

Despite its unattractive English name (the Spanish means 'little knots from Zamora'), this is one of my favourite desserts. Sweet and chewy with a tang of cinnamon, it is very popular throughout Mexico.

4 pints (2.4 litres) milk
12 oz (350 g) granulated sugar
5 teaspoons (5 × 5 ml spoon) rennet essence
6-inch (15 cm) piece of cinnamon stick

Heat the milk and sugar in a saucepan to body temperature, 98°F/36°C, then stir in the rennet essence. Leave overnight in a warm place until set (it sets like jelly and looks quite firm).

The next day, cut the curd into 1-inch (2.5 cm) squares with a very pointed knife. Break the cinnamon stick into small pieces and insert a piece into each square.

Now simmer for 4 hours on the lowest possible heat. It must only just bubble, because the curds disintegrate easily if boiled hard. After 4 hours remove the curds, then boil the liquid quickly for 15 minutes until it reduces by half. Pour the syrup over the curds and allow to cool. Refrigerate and serve cold.

Dulce de Calabaza en Tacha

Stewed pumpkin in sugar syrup
Serves 6

In Mexico, pumpkin is mostly eaten as a dessert, not a vegetable. Try both ways of making this dessert – with granulated sugar and with muscavado sugar. The flavours are quite different.

2 pints (1.2 litres) water
juice and coarsely chopped rind of 2 oranges
1½ lb (675 g) raw pumpkin, cut into six and punctured on all sides with a fork.
1½ lb (675 g) granulated or muscavado sugar
4-inch (8 cm) piece of cinnamon stick or 2 teaspoons (2 × 5 ml spoon) powdered cinnamon

Place the water in a 5-pint (3-litre) saucepan and add the orange juice and rind. Boil until the rind is soft. Add the pumpkin, sugar and cinnamon. Simmer until the pumpkin is soft. Remove it and boil the remaining mixture for another 30–40 minutes or until it is reduced to half the original amount.

Return the pumpkin to the syrup and simmer for a further 5 minutes. Remove the cinnamon stick if used. Allow to cool and then refrigerate. Serve well chilled.

Dulce de Calabaza en Tacha and Chocolate Caliente

Buñuelos
Crispy pancakes with sugar and cinnamon
Serves 4

Buñuelos, which originated in southern Mexico, are especially good with a warm muscavado sugar syrup. There are many ways of preparing them, some of which are too complicated and time-consuming. The one I have chosen for this book is a very practical and tasty recipe, which is eaten mainly in the north and is very good with coffee or as a sweet biscuit for tea-time.

oil for deep frying
4 fresh or frozen wheat flour tortillas
4 oz (100 g) caster sugar
1 teaspoon (5 ml spoon) powdered cinnamon

Heat the oil to about 375°F/190°C. Defrost the tortillas for 20 minutes if they are frozen. Cut each tortilla into 8 pieces. Immerse half of the tortillas (16 pieces) at a time in the hot oil for about 1 minute, stirring occasionally so that they brown evenly. Put the caster sugar and cinnamon in a paper bag. When the tortillas are golden brown, remove with a slotted spoon and shake each batch gently in the paper bag. Arrange on a plate and serve when cool.

Cajeta

Milk caramel
Serves 8

This treacle-like mixture is very popular. Traditionally made from goat's milk, it is sold commercially in large jars. The children fill their spoons and then lick them at leisure! It is also served on vanilla ice cream or can be mixed with a little rum as a filling for French crêpes, garnished with chopped nuts.

2 pints (1.2 litres) milk
12 oz (350 g) granulated sugar
¼ teaspoon (1.25 ml spoon) bicarbonate of soda
½ teaspoon (2.5 ml spoon) powdered cinnamon or 5-inch (10 cm)
    piece of cinnamon stick

Place ½ pint (300 ml) of the milk and all the sugar in a 4-pint (2.4 litre) saucepan and bring to the boil. Simmer for about 20 minutes until the milk goes a rich brown, then remove from heat.

Pour the rest of the milk into another saucepan with the bicarbonate of soda and cinnamon and bring to the boil. Then add this very, very slowly (it rises very fast) to the sugar and milk mixture, and stir or whip with a wire whisk for a few minutes to dissolve any brown sugar specks.

Place the mixture back on a low heat, skim any froth that comes to the surface, and simmer, stirring only occasionally, for 1 hour or more, until it reaches 225°F/120°C on a sugar thermometer. Pour into a warmed, clean jar and allow to cool. Eat cold with sweet biscuits or use as suggested above.

Bebidas
Drinks

Mexicans love hot chocolate – but they are also very fond of fresh, cool fruit drinks, which are always on the Mexican table. Limeade, made with the juice of freshly squeezed limes, orangeade or diluted grapefruit or pineapple juice and sorrel water, a brilliant red tea made with a wild blossom, are all very popular. The colours of such drinks range from white through to a dark brown, which is obtained from the bitter-sweet tamarind fruit.

Mexico has, of course, made its name with the famous aperitif tequila, known as 'fire water', which is always accompanied by lime juice and salt to extinguish the fire! A well-known tequila manufacturer in Mexico recommends the lime first, then salt and finally a one-ounce shot of tequila, but customs vary and so you should experiment to see in which order you like them best.

I should also mention *Cafe de Olla*, or Mexican coffee. Coffee is drunk mostly black in rural Mexico, the beans having been gathered in the wild or grown on home allotments and then home roasted. They are often not of very good quality and the addition of raw cane sugar (muscavado) and cinnamon to the boiling coffee disguises any impurities and turns it into quite a delicious drink.

Margaritas
Tequila cocktails (pictured on p. 45)

The most popular cocktail with a real Mexican bang. It always surprises the uninitiated as the taste of the salted rim of the glass hits them first. In fact, it is a very practical way of serving tequila, which would otherwise be served with quartered limes and coarse salt. For two cocktails you need:

1 lime or lemon
4 fl oz (110 ml) white tequila
2 tablespoons (2 × 15 ml spoon) Triple Sec or Cointreau
4 ice cubes

Halve the lime or lemon and rub the rim of each cocktail glass with one of the halves. Then dip each glass into a saucer full of the salt and chill the glass in the refrigerator.

Squeeze out the juice of the other half of the lime or lemon and blend at high speed for 30 seconds with the tequila, the liqueur and ice cubes. Pour into the chilled glasses and serve. (It is not advisable to prepare Margaritas more than half an hour ahead of time, because the lime goes bitter.)

Ponche de Tequila
Tequila party punch
Makes 20 drinks

Tequila has the advantage over other drinks of getting parties going very soon after people arrive. It is very strong and breaks the ice, so to speak, almost immediately. In fact the tequila that is exported has to be made separately, as the Mexican proof is too high for other countries! This punch can be prepared before the party starts, while you're still capable!

1 large bottle (750 ml) tequila
8 oz (225 g) granulated sugar
juice of 6 oranges
juice of 6 limes or lemons
2 × 500 ml bottles of American dry ginger
2 × 500 ml bottles of soda water
40 ice cubes

Mix all the ingredients except the ice together vigorously and chill for 1 hour. Put 2 ice cubes in each glass and pour the punch over them.

Cafe de Olla
Mexican coffee

Cafe de Olla is popular amongst the Mexican peasants, who brew it in earthenware pots and serve it in small earthenware mugs. It is a convenient way of using any leftover coffee. Although the coffee is generally boiled with the sugar and the cinnamon, this method often makes it go bitter, and so I prefer to make the syrup separately and add it to the coffee as desired. For 2 cups of coffee you need:

a 4-inch (10 cm) piece of cinnamon stick or ½ teaspoon (2.5 ml
  spoon) powdered cinnamon
4 teaspoons (4 × 5 ml spoon) muscavado sugar
3 tablespoons (3 × 15 ml spoon) water

Boil all the ingredients together for 3 minutes and pour into the hot coffee or serve hot in a separate jug.

Chocolate Caliente

Mexican hot chocolate (pictured on p. 89)
Serves 4

A drink given daily to children for breakfast and supper. Traditionally it is drunk hot after being whisked with a 'molinillo'. This very typical Mexican kitchen utensil is a type of wooden whisk, carved all in one piece, with rings carved out of it in different sizes (it appears in the photograph on p. 9).

4 oz (100 g) plain chocolate or unsweetened cooking chocolate, grated
1 pint (600 ml) milk
2 oz (50 g) granulated sugar
2 drops of vanilla essence
1 tablespoon (15 ml spoon) cornflour
4 tablespoons (4 × 15 ml spoon) cold water
a sprinkling of powdered cinnamon

Place the chocolate, milk, sugar and vanilla in a saucepan and warm gently, stirring constantly. Do not allow it to boil. Dissolve the cornflour in the cold water and add slowly to the milk, stirring constantly. Give it a good whisk to form bubbles and serve hot, sprinkled with the ground cinnamon

The Author

Lourdes Nichols was born in Mexico City and has lived in England for the last fifteen years. She began cooking at an early age, learning from her mother, who also helped her in compiling the recipes in this book.

When she first came to England Lourdes found it difficult to adapt her native Mexican recipes to the ingredients then available, although the choice of produce has improved considerably since. For the past four years she has been seriously involved in researching and teaching Mexican cookery.

Lourdes now divides her time between teaching, writing and catering for parties at the Mexican Embassy, Mexican Tourist Board and elsewhere, as well as running a small commercial tortilla-making business. She is a recognised authority on Mexican cuisine and has been featured on BBC TV's *Pebble Mill at One* and Radio 4's *Food Programme*.

Lourdes lives in the Home Counties with her English husband and their three teenage children, who she says have been very encouraging and willing to try endless recipes!